Cool Careers
in Science

▸ Fighting internet
bad guys

▸ Protecting
companies and
governments

▸ Key skills for
success

Professional
HACKERS

ALTERNATIVE REALITY DEVELOPERS

ARTIFICIAL INTELLIGENCE SCIENTISTS

COMPUTER GAME & APP DEVELOPERS

DRIVERLESS VEHICLE DEVELOPERS

DRONE PILOTS

ENTERTAINMENT ENGINEERS

FORENSIC SCIENTISTS

PROFESSIONAL HACKERS

RENEWABLE ENERGY WORKERS

ROBOTICS DEVELOPERS

Cool Careers
in Science

Professional
HACKERS

ANDREW MORKES

MASON CREST
PHILADELPHIA
MIAMI

Mason Crest
450 Parkway Drive, Suite D
Broomall, Pennsylvania 19008
(866) MCP-BOOK (toll-free)

First printing

9 8 7 6 5 4 3 2 1

HARDBACK ISBN: 978-1-4222-4300-8
SERIES ISBN: 978-1-4222-4292-6
E-BOOK ISBN: 978-1-4222-7517-7

Cataloging-in-Publication Data on file with the Library of Congress

Developed and Produced by National Highlights, Inc.
Interior and cover design: Jana Rade, impact studios
Interior layout: Annalisa Gumbrecht, Studio Gumbrecht
Production: Michelle Luke
Proofreader: Susan Uttendorfsky

QR CODES AND LINKS TO THIRD-PARTY CONTENT

Table of Contents

KEY ICONS TO LOOK FOR:

 WORDS TO UNDERSTAND: These words with their easy-to-understand definitions will increase the reader's understanding of the text while building vocabulary skills.

 SIDEBARS: This boxed material within the main text allows readers to build knowledge, gain insights, explore possibilities, and broaden their perspectives by weaving together additional information to provide realistic and holistic perspectives.

 EDUCATIONAL VIDEOS: Readers can view videos by scanning our QR codes, providing them with additional educational content to supplement the text. Examples include news coverage, moments in history, speeches, iconic sports moments, and much more!

 TEXT-DEPENDENT QUESTIONS: These questions send the reader back to the text for more careful attention to the evidence presented there.

 RESEARCH PROJECTS: Readers are pointed toward areas of further inquiry connected to each chapter. Suggestions are provided for projects that encourage deeper research and analysis.

CAREERS IN SCIENCE OFFER GOOD PAY, THE OPPORTUNITY TO HELP PEOPLE, AND OTHER REWARDS

Where would we be without science? Well, we'd be without computers, smartphones, and other cutting-edge technologies. Crimes would take longer to solve without modern forensic analysis techniques. More of our private information would be stolen by hackers. We'd be stuck relying on environmentally unfriendly fossil fuels instead of using renewable energy. And life would be less fun because we wouldn't have drones, awe-inspiring and physics-defying roller coasters, and the computer and video games that we play for hours and hours.

Job markets are sometimes strong and sometimes weak, but a career in science (which, for the purposes of this series, includes the related fields of technology and engineering) is almost a sure path to a comfortable life. The following paragraphs provide more information on why a career in science is a great choice.

Good pay. People in science careers earn some of the highest salaries in the work world. Median annual salaries for those in computer and mathematical careers in the United States are $84,575, according to the U.S. Department of Labor (USDL). This is much higher than the median earnings ($37,690) for all careers. Additionally, those in life, physical, and social science occupations can earn $64,510, and those in engineering careers earn $79,180. Science professionals who become managers or who launch their own businesses can earn anywhere from $150,000 to $300,000 or more.

Strong employment prospects. There are shortages of science workers throughout the world, according to the consulting firm ManpowerGroup. In fact, engineering workers are the third most in demand occupational field in the world. Technicians rank fourth, and computer and information technology professionals rank sixth.

There's a shortage of software engineers in more than twenty countries, including in the United States, Canada, Mexico, Japan, and the United Kingdom, according to the recruitment firm Michael Page. Other science careers where there is a shortage of workers include electronics engineers (nineteen countries), electrical engineers (sixteen countries), data analysts (eleven countries), and hardware engineers (six countries), among other workers.

The USDL predicts that employment of computer and information technology professionals in the United States will grow by 13 percent during the next decade. Career opportunities for those in life, physical, and social science occupations will grow by 10 percent. Both of these career fields are growing faster than the average for all careers. The outlook is also good for engineering professionals. Employment is expected to grow by 7 percent during the next decade. The strongest opportunities will be found in renewable energy and robotics.

By 2026, the USDL predicts that there will be more than 876,000 new jobs in science, technology, engineering, and mathematics fields.

Rewarding work environment and many career options. A career in science is fulfilling because you get to use both your creative and practical sides to develop new technologies (or improve existing ones), solve problems, and make the world a better place. There's a common misconception that science workers spend most of their time in dreary, windowless laboratories. While they do spend lots of time in the laboratory, they also spend time in the field, testing, troubleshooting, and trying out their inventions or discoveries. Some science professionals launch their own businesses, which can be both fun and very rewarding.

Job opportunities are available throughout the United States and the world. Science professionals play such an important role in our modern world that there are jobs almost anywhere, although many positions are found in big cities.

IS A CAREER IN SCIENCE RIGHT FOR ME?

Test your interest. How many of these statements do you agree with?

_____ My favorite class in school is science.

_____ I also enjoy computer science classes.

_____ I like to learn about scientific breakthroughs.

_____ I like to build and fix things.

_____ I enjoy doing science experiments.

_____ I enjoy coming up with ideas on how to solve the world's problems.

_____ I am curious about how things work.

_____ I like to invent things.

_____ I am creative and have a good imagination.

_____ I like to build electronics and other things that require electricity.

_____ I am good at math.

If many of the statements above describe you, then you should consider a career in the sciences. But you don't need to select a career right now. Check out this book on a career as a professional hacker, and other books in the series, to learn more about occupational paths in the sciences and related fields. Good luck with your career exploration!

WORDS TO UNDERSTAND

intellectual property: creations of the human mind, such as inventions, designs, and artistic and literary works

Internet of Things: a network of appliances, vehicles, etc., that are embedded with electronics, sensors, software, and other technology that allows them to communicate with each other and share information

open source software: a type of software that is free and which anyone can inspect, modify, and improve the code that makes it work

sabotage: to deliberately obstruct, damage, or destroy something

server: a computer that processes requests and delivers data to another computer over a local network or the internet

Chapter 1

WHAT DO PROFESSIONAL HACKERS DO?

WHAT ARE DIGITAL SECURITY AND COMPUTER HACKING?

Technology is everywhere these days—from our laptops and smartphones to the software that's used to operate everything from our cars to massive assembly lines in manufacturing plants. If you think about it, there are few places where technology—including the internet—is not used in some way or another.

Advances in technology make life easier and help people to become more connected. A task that used to take days can now be done in a matter of minutes with a computer. Before computers, the internet, and the telephone, it would take days—or even weeks—for people across the country or world to communicate. Email, instant messaging, texting, and other digital communication methods now allow people who live thousands of miles away from each other to communicate in real-time. Technology is also used to save lives. In the old days, people could become very ill or even die if they had an abnormal heart rhythm. Today, a pacemaker, which uses electrical pulses

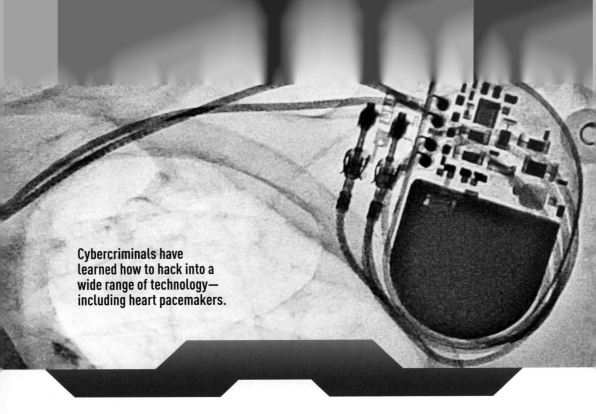

Cybercriminals have learned how to hack into a wide range of technology—including heart pacemakers.

to prompt the heart to beat at a normal rate, can be placed in the chest or abdomen of a patient to help control abnormal heart rhythms.

Overall, technology is a good thing. But there is also a dark side to the increasing use of technology. There are people who want to steal our personal information and hack into our social media accounts and post lies about us, or cause other types of trouble. There are also people or groups that try to break into government databases and systems, steal financial information from companies, destroy data or information systems, or create other problems. Others might even seek to harm us by using the cars we drive or the medical technology that is implanted in us. For example, a hacker could take advantage of security flaws in a pacemaker to deliver shocks to the heart when they aren't needed, or withhold shocks when they are needed. This could cause a person to get sick or even die.

The people who use technology to steal our personal information, **sabotage** computer systems, or even tamper with pacemakers are known as "black hat hackers" or "cybercriminals." Professional hackers, who are also known as *white hat hackers, ethical hackers,* and *information security analysts* (although people with this job title many have other non-hacking duties) are the good guys and girls. They try to stop cybercriminals from hacking into people's computers and committing other cybercrimes. Professional hackers may also have specialized job duties based on their job duties. For example, *incident analysts* and *responders* seek to learn as much as possible about an ongoing cyberattack, and then attempt to stop it. *Penetration* and *vulnerability testers* seek to hack into an organization's computer systems—with permission—to see if they are at risk of being hacked by cybercriminals. But more about the work of professional hackers in a bit.

Government cybersecurity experts have detected attempted cyberattacks on nuclear power plants and other types of energy infrastructure.

THE EFFECTS OF CYBERCRIME

There are many negative effects of cybercrime, including:

- Damage or destruction to data
- Theft of money
- Theft of **intellectual property**
- Loss of personal or financial data
- Damage to one's reputation
- Disruption to one's daily or work life
- Physical harm or death to an individual
- The cost of restoring damaged or destroyed systems
- Destruction of public utilities (water, electric, natural gas, telecommunications systems)
- Weakening of a country's military, defense system, or reputation

All these negative effects make it even more important that we have highly skilled professional hackers to protect us from cybercrime.

WHY WHITE HATS AND BLACK HATS?

Professional hackers are known as white hat hackers because the good guys in old Western television shows and movies typically wore white cowboy hats, while the bad guys wore black cowboy hats.

TYPES OF CYBERATTACKS

There are many types of cyberattacks. Cisco, a worldwide leader in information technology and networking, identifies the following as the most common methods of cyberattack.

MALWARE

Malware is a term that is used to describe software—including spyware, ransomware, worms, and viruses—that are created to harm computers or other types of technology. Malware is activated when a user unknowingly clicks a seemingly harmless link or email attachment, or plugs in a flash drive or other type of external storage device. Once activated, the malware causes many problems, including:

- Acting as ransomware and blocking access to certain files, the main components of the network, or entire computers or systems
- Installing even more harmful software
- Using spyware to collect and transmit data from the hard drive to the cybercriminal at a remote location

DID YOU KNOW?

- In 2018, more than 4,000 ransomware attacks occurred each day— a 300 percent increase from 2015.
- The total amount of ransomware payments approaches $1 billion annually.
- Cybercriminals create an average of 1.4 million phishing websites each month.
- It's estimated that one in every 131 emails contains malware.
- In the first half of 2016, more than 3 million data records were lost or stolen.

Sources: Federal Bureau of Investigation, CyberArk

More than 4,000 ransomware
attacks occurred each day in 2018.

PHISHING

In a phishing attack, a cybercriminal sends an email or another type of digital communication that appears to come from a trustworthy source. When the recipient clicks on a link in the email, malware is activated and used to steal sensitive data (such as credit card and login information) or to commit other crimes. Seventy-six percent of information security professionals surveyed by Wombat Security (a security awareness and training software company) revealed that their organization had experienced phishing attacks in 2017.

MAN-IN-THE-MIDDLE ATTACKS

In this type of attack, a cybercriminal finds a way to access an individual's or organization's computer to steal data. For example, if a user is connecting to the internet in a public place over an unsecured connection, the cybercriminal can interrupt the connection between the two parties and steal information. Another way to conduct a man-in-the-middle attack, which is also known as an eavesdropping attack, is to use malware to gain access to an individual's or organization's computer system. Every time a user provides credit card information to make a purchase, for example, the cybercriminal uses the malware to steal the credit card number.

Since teens are frequent users of the internet and other technology, they are often victims of cybercrime.

TEENS, TECHNOLOGY, AND SOCIAL MEDIA

In 2018, the Pew Research Center conducted a survey of teens aged thirteen to seventeen to try to better understand their use of technology. Here are some results from the survey:

- 95 percent of teens reported that they had a smartphone, or access to one.

- 45 percent said that they were online on a near-constant basis.

- 85 percent reported that they used YouTube. The second most popular social media site was Instagram (used by 72 percent of those surveyed), followed by Snapchat (69 percent), Facebook (51 percent), and Twitter (32 percent).

DENIAL-OF-SERVICE ATTACK

This type of attack overwhelms networks, systems, and **servers** with so much traffic that there is little or no bandwidth to provide regular services. (Bandwidth is the amount of data that can be sent from one point to another in a certain amount of time.) A distributed-denial-of-service (DDoS) attack occurs when cybercriminals use multiple compromised devices to launch an attack. In May 2017, 85 percent of organizations surveyed by the information services firm Neusta had experienced a DDoS attack within the past year. Eighty-six percent of those companies had been attacked more than once.

STRUCTURED QUERY LANGUAGE INJECTION

This type of attack occurs when a cybercriminal inserts malicious, or harmful, code (instructions that tell a computer what to do) into a server that uses Structured Query Language (SQL). SQL is a programming language that is used to store, manipulate, and retrieve data in servers and databases. This code forces the server to provide information that is normally protected from hackers. One example of an SQL injection involves a cybercriminal submitting malicious code into a vulnerable website search box to hack a system.

ZERO-DAY EXPLOIT ATTACK

Cybercriminals initiate this type of attack after a software developer announces that it has detected a network vulnerability in one of its products, but before the problem can be addressed. (A vulnerability is a bug, back door, or glitch in an operating system, firmware, or software that can be exploited, or taken advantage of, by a cybercriminal.) That's why it's very important that professional hackers identify vulnerabilities before they can be exploited by cybercriminals.

CYBERCRIME DOESN'T PAY

It might seem exciting to break the rules and earn a little extra money as a black hat hacker. But think twice before going over to the dark side of hacking. Federal, state, and local governments are expanding their cybercrime departments and cracking down on teens who commit cybercrimes—even if their goal was just to have a little fun. Here are some recent examples from CSOonline.com and other sources that show that cybercrime does not pay:

- A seventeen-year-old was sentenced to twelve months of rehabilitation after using an iPhone to hack a British telecommunications company.

- A Canadian teen who hacked U.S. federal agencies is serving a four-year prison sentence.

- In California, the Secret Service and local police arrested a teenager who used a phishing scam to break into his high school's computer system to raise, and even drop, the grades of ten to fifteen students.

- A teen in Virginia may be required to serve fifteen months in federal prison and repay $36,240 for breaking into computers from the U.S. Information Agency and two businesses.

Some teens may think it's okay to use computers to change school grades or cause other problems, but some cyber pranksters have been sentenced to jail time for their actions.

EXAMPLES OF CYBERSECURITY ATTACKS

If you still don't think cyberattacks are a big deal, here are some examples of recent major cybersecurity attacks that affected millions of people.

- 2015: Anthem, a health care insurance provider, announced that hackers had stolen the personal information of 78.8 million customers.

- 2016: Hackers stole the data of 57 million Uber customers.

- 2017: The credit monitoring firm Equifax reported that cybercriminals had stolen the personal information of 145.5 million people, including birth dates, addresses, and some driver's license numbers; Social Security numbers of about half the U.S. population; and about 209,000 credit card numbers.

- 2018: The U.S. government announced that Russian hackers had broken into and were probing the computer systems of U.S. power companies. Authorities worry that the Russian hackers might be able to take control of these systems and cause them to stop working or malfunction.

- 2018: Nine Iranian hackers were indicted (to charge with a serious crime) for breaking into the information technology systems of 144 U.S. universities, 176 universities in 21 other countries, 47 private companies, and other targets, such as the states of Hawaii and Indiana and the United Nations. The U.S. Department of Justice reported that the hackers stole intellectual property that was estimated to be worth $3 billion.

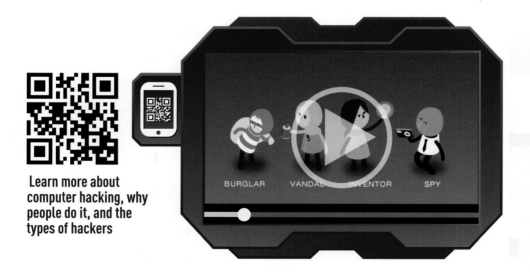

Learn more about computer hacking, why people do it, and the types of hackers

BURGLAR   VANDAL   INVENTOR   SPY

DAY IN THE LIFE: PROFESSIONAL HACKER AT A SOFTWARE COMPANY

I'm a professional hacker for a well-known software company. Before I tell you about my work, let me bust some common stereotypes about hackers. I don't wear a black hoodie. I don't consider myself a nerd. I don't play video games 24/7. I even get outside sometimes in the sunshine, and I like a good hike. I love computers, but I'm not obsessed with them. In short, I'm just a regular person who is interested in computers and wants to protect people from black hat hackers—the bad guys.

I became interested in hacking in high school. I'd play these online games and try to hack into the system to get free plays, or weapons and powers for my character. In college, I took a few classes in computer security, including one on ethical hacking. I was majoring in software development, but I switched my major to cybersecurity because I was much more interested in assessing systems for vulnerabilities and fighting off cyberattacks than developing software (although software development is certainly part of my job).

I basically work in the forensics area of professional hacking. I look at logs from intrusion detection and prevention systems and look for clues to how the hacker accessed our software. Then I try to recreate the hacking scenario. I seek answers to questions such as, "How did the hacker get into the system?", "What methods/tools were used?", and "What happened after the hack occurred?" Then I develop a plan to stop this from happening again.

I also do penetration testing. I go to the customer's website and initiate attacks. Of course, the customer knows exactly what I'm doing beforehand. I'll check the site's firewall status, and I'll introduce malware to see if the customer's security software and hardware can block my attack. I also use social engineering techniques. My goal is to learn about key players at the company and send phishing emails to trick them into clicking on links that contain malware. I'll spoof an email account and pretend I'm a coworker to get them to provide private information.

If an outbreak, or attack, occurs, I have to work quickly to find the root causes—where the infection is occurring and how it's being spread. This is the most exciting part of the job because I have to think quickly to stop the hacker from doing damage. It's exciting to thwart an attack. If you like computers, solving problems, and the occasional adrenaline-filled day, you'll love working as a professional hacker.

PROFESSIONAL HACKERS

The science television show *NOVA* defines computer hacking as "creative problem-solving that takes advantage of the properties of computers and networks in unexpected ways." Hacking is a word that makes people think of cyberattacks, but hacking can be both positive and negative. Think of hacking like a tool, such as a hammer. People can use a hammer to either build or destroy something. Hacking is the same way. It can be used for both good and evil.

Professional hackers are skilled computer professionals who use hacking to do good. They attempt to stop cyberattacks before they happen. They also try to stop or reduce the damage of attacks that occur in real-time. Cybercrime is a major problem in the U.S. and throughout the world. CNBC.com reports that "cyber theft is the fastest-growing crime in the United States and cost the global economy more than $450 billion in 2016, with more than 2 billion

Professional hackers play a key role in preventing cyberattacks.

personal records stolen." As a result, the demand for professional hackers is extremely strong.

Professional hackers receive permission from government agencies, companies, and individuals to hack into software applications, mobile devices, web services, network systems, devices connected via the **Internet of Things**, and other types of technology. They either work for these organizations and individuals directly, or they are hired as freelancers. A freelancer is a type of worker who does not work full time for a company or organization but who provides services as needed. Freelancers do not receive a regular salary, but are paid by the hour or project.

Duties for professional hackers vary by type of employer, educational background, and job title, but the following paragraphs provide information on some of their most important responsibilities.

When first starting an assignment, a professional hacker studies a customer's technology systems to identify security flaws and vulnerabilities. They use their vast knowledge of network systems, networking systems, operating systems hardware platforms—and the security vulnerabilities within each category—to identify areas of risk. Their goal is to think like cybercriminals.

Professional hackers then use commercial and **open source** hacking software to conduct simulated attacks (called "penetration testing," or "pentests") on the systems. Some of the most common attack methods include malware, phishing, man-in-the-middle attacks, denial-of-service attacks, and Structured Query Language injections.

After they've successfully hacked a system—or have been stopped by an organization's firewall (the part of a computer or network that blocks unauthorized access while allowing outward communication from the user) and professional hackers—they prepare a report that details their findings and suggests ways for organizations to improve their security. Some professional hackers record their hacking sessions so that they can show employers exactly what they did to access the systems.

A professional hacker works closely with software developers, hardware engineers, and other computer professionals to fix the issues. They may create custom software or systems to help organizations solve these issues. Once the new security suggestions have been set up, the professional hacker retests the system to ensure it cannot be breached, or broken into.

It might be surprising to learn that not all penetration testing strategies are digital. A comprehensive pentest involves actually testing the physical security of a facility. After all, critical data can also be downloaded and stolen by someone who sneaks into a company. A cybercriminal might also sneak into a military base and not steal anything, but sabotage a computer network. In this type of penetration testing, a professional hacker attempts to get into a secure building. They might simply travel to a facility and try to climb a security gate, or check to see if a door was left unlocked. They also attempt to talk their way into a facility by saying that they've forgotten their security badge or code, or they may dress in an expensive suit and pretend that they work as an executive at the company. Some professional hackers might even tailgate another car through an access gate to get in.

Professional hackers have other duties, including:

- Monitoring computer systems on a daily basis to ensure that they are working correctly and that no one is trying to hack into the systems
- Setting up security policies that keep systems safe

- Training workers regarding best practices for network security
- Staying up-to-date on the latest testing tools and techniques, as well as current trends in cybercrime

PROFESSIONAL HACKER CAREER PATH

Hard work and talent are rewarded in the cybersecurity field. Within a few years of hard work, you can advance to a managerial position, or even start your own cybersecurity business. Here is a typical career ladder for professional hackers:

Business Owner

Director of Cybersecurity

Cybersecurity Engineer

Professional Hacker

Cybersecurity Student

TEXT-DEPENDENT QUESTIONS:

1. What is malware?
2. What is the difference between a professional hacker and black hat hacker?
3. What happened when Equifax was hacked?

RESEARCH PROJECT:

Learn more about the most common types of cyberattacks that were discussed in this chapter. Write a report that provides more information on each, and what you can do to avoid them. Present this information to your computer class.

Chapter 2

TERMS OF THE TRADE

anti-virus software: Computer software that is designed to stop viruses from attacking computers and other technology.

attribution: The process of determining who committed a cybercrime.

backdoor access: An attempt by a cybercriminal to find unprotected pathways into a computer system.

bandwidth: The amount of data that can be sent from one point to another in a certain amount of time.

black hat hacker: An individual who uses their technical and hacking skills for personal gain (money or fame), and/or to commit a crime.

bot: Malicious software that is secretly installed on a computer that allows a cybercriminal to use it to commit a distributed-denial-of-service attack, send spam, or commit other crimes.

brandjacking: A type of cybercrime in which criminals create a fake website or email message that looks like it was created/produced by a respected company; financial institutions, utilities, media companies, and telecommunications firms are often brandjacked.

bug: A glitch or problem with software; some bugs can be exploited by cybercriminals if they are not fixed by the software developer.

bug bounty: Money paid to professional hackers or everyday computer users if they find a bug before the bad guys do.

catfishing: The process of creating a fake online identity to trick people into emotional or romantic relationships; an individual who has been catfished may be tricked into giving personal or financial information or blackmailed (pressured) to provide money so that their actions won't be revealed to people they care about.

code: Instructions that tell a computer what to do.

compromised device: A computer or other type of technology that is completely or partially controlled by a cybercriminal.

confidentiality: Making sure that information is available only to those who have permission to use it.

cracking: The process of breaking into a security system by a cybercriminal.

cryptocurrency: Digital money.

cryptography: The study of methods for scrambling or rearranging data in order to disguise it when it is transmitted between two or more parties.

cyber-espionage: The act of using the internet or other technology to steal classified or sensitive data or intellectual property to gain an advantage over a company or government.

dark web: An alternative area of the internet that is not indexed (organized) by Google and that is only accessible through specialty networks such as Tor. The dark web is used by people, often cybercriminals, who want to remain anonymous.

data breach: When information is stolen by cybercriminals.

decryption: The process of decoding data or messages that were encrypted.

deep web: The part of the internet that is not indexed by search engines (it includes paywalled sites, encrypted networks, password-protected pages, and databases). The deep web is estimated to be as much as 5,000 times larger than the surface web.

denial-of-service attack: A cyberattack that seeks to overwhelm networks, systems, and servers with so much traffic that there is little or no bandwidth to provide regular services.

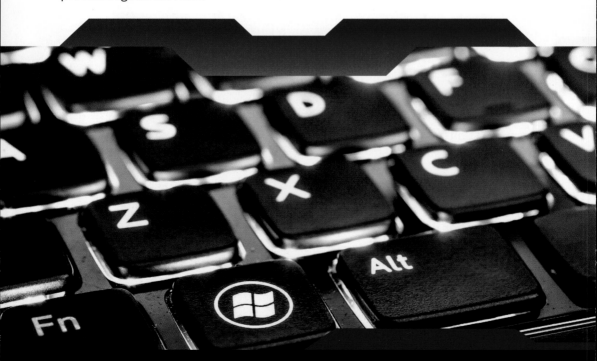

distributed-denial-of-service (DDoS): A denial-of-service attack that occurs when cybercriminals use multiple compromised devices to launch an attack.

encryption: The process of digitally scrambling (mixing up) data or messages in order to make them secret and unreadable. Corporations, government agencies, and individuals use encryption to keep their data or messages safe from cybercriminals; it is a subfield of cryptography.

exploit: To take advantage of a bug or other vulnerability on a computer or network.

firewall: The part of a computer or network that blocks unauthorized access while allowing outward communication from the user.

firmware: Software that tells hardware what to do.

footprinting: Gathering information about computer systems and the larger systems they are connected to in order to get clues on how to hack a system.

hacker: The term for both people who seek to use their computer and hacking skills to do good, and those who use their talents to do bad.

hacktivist: A person or organization (such as Anonymous) that uses their hacking skills for political ends. Hacktivists do everything from simply defacing (damaging) or shutting down the website of a government agency or corporation to stealing secret government information and giving it to the public.

keylogging: Using malicious software that records or logs the keys that an individual strikes on a keyboard in order to capture private information or communications; also known as **keystroke logging** and **keyboard capturing**.

malicious: Deliberately harmful.

malware: A term used to describe software, including spyware, ransomware, Trojan horses, adware, worms, and viruses that have been created to harm computers or other technology.

man-in-the-middle attack: A type of attack in which a cybercriminal finds a way to access an individual's or organization's computer (via a public, unprotected wireless network, for example) to steal data or cause other harm.

network: A group of computers.

open source software: A type of software that is free and which anyone can inspect, modify, and improve the code that makes it work.

penetration testing: The process of attempting to break into a computer system to make sure that there are no vulnerabilities that would make it easy to hack by cybercriminals; also known as **pentesting**.

phishing attack: Occurs when a cybercriminal sends an email or another type of digital communication that appears to come from a trustworthy source (friend, family member, customer service representative at Google, etc.) in order to steal sensitive data such as credit card and login information, or commit other crimes.

ransomware: A type of malware that infects and locks a user's computer so that they can't access it. Cybercriminals offer to unlock the device if the person pays a ransom (the money is usually requested in cryptocurrency) that ranges from a few hundred dollars to $20,000 or more.

red team: A group of professional hackers who are hired by companies or other organizations to attack their computer systems and try to take them over. The goal of the red team is to identify security issues before they are taken advantage of by cybercriminals.

risk factor: The probability that something bad will happen.

server: A computer that processes requests and delivers data to another computer over a local network or the internet.

script kiddie: A negative term for amateurs who download and attempt to use hacking tools without any skill at doing so.

sniffer: A software program that monitors and analyzes network traffic in order to detect and fix problems. A sniffer can be used by network managers to keep traffic moving and identify issues before they become major problems, but it can also be used by black hat hackers to steal data being transmitted on a network.

social engineering: The process of convincing a computer user via an email, instant message, phone call, or an interaction in person to provide information (or click on a link in the digital message) that will allow a cybercriminal to hack into a system.

software: A program that operates a computer or allows a user to perform a specific task.

spear fishing: A type of phishing that is more targeted; cybercriminals gather detailed information about the victim that allows them to better target them and gain their confidence.

spyware: A type of malware that is used to spy on the actions of computer users and steal data or other types of information.

SQL: Stands for Structured Query Language; a programming language that is used to store, manipulate, and retrieve data in servers and databases.

state actor: A hacker or group of cybercriminals who are supported and funded by a government.

SQL injection: A cyberattack in which a cybercriminal inserts malicious code into a server that uses SQL to force the server to provide information that is normally protected from hackers.

threat: Any person or action that can take advantage of a vulnerability.

Trojan horse: Code that is hidden in a computer file or program that causes harm when activated.

virus: A type of malware that is typically hidden in a software program or computer file; it must be downloaded or forwarded for it to be activated.

vulnerability: A bug, back door, or glitch in an operating system, firmware, or software that can be exploited by a cybercriminal.

whaling: A type of email fraud that targets executives or high-level managers at a company with a goal of convincing them to provide private information. The email looks like it is from someone the individual knows, which causes the executive to click on a link that contains malware, or provide sensitive information.

white hat hacker: An individual who uses their technical and hacking skills for good—to help companies detect security issues, help government agencies fight cybercriminals, and perform other positive activities.

worm: A type of malware that reproduces automatically without a computer user doing anything. Once it becomes active, it spreads from computer to computer.

zero-day exploit attack: A cyberattack in which a hacker attacks a compromised system before it can be fixed.

zombie armies: Networks of computers that have been infected with malware and taken over and controlled by cyberattacks; zombie armies, which are also known as **botnets**, can be used to create DDoS attacks.

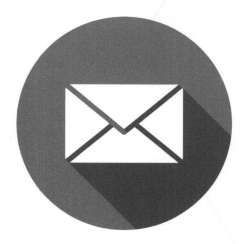

WORDS TO UNDERSTAND

internship: a paid or unpaid learning opportunity in which a student works at a business to get experience; it can last anywhere from a few weeks to a year

professional association: an organization that is founded by a group of people who have the same career (engineers, professional hackers, scientists, etc.) or who work in the same industry specialty (information technology, health care, etc.)

registered apprenticeships: programs that meet standards of fairness, safety, and training established by the U.S. government or local governments

resume: a formal summary of one's educational and work experience that is submitted to a potential employer

Chapter 3

PREPARING FOR THE FIELD AND MAKING A LIVING

EDUCATIONAL PATHS

There are several ways to train for a career as a professional hacker. Many hackers have bachelors and masters degrees in computer security, computer science, software development, network administration, or related fields. Some people earn certificates in ethical hacking and an associate's degree in computer security. Others get their training in the military or through a short apprenticeship. A few people who are whizzes with technology even enter the field after high school, but that entry path is becoming rare because employers want applicants who have completed at least some post–high school training. The following sections provide more information on educational preparation.

Take as many computer science classes as possible in high school to prepare for the field.

HIGH SCHOOL CLASSES

As a teenager, you're probably already completely immersed in the world of social media, *Fortnite* or other computer games, YouTube channels, smartphones, and other types of technology and online fun. But you should also use this time to take as many computer science classes as possible. Some recommended classes include:

- Introduction to Computer Science
- Computer Programming
- Software Development
- Computer Networking
- Database Management
- Computer Security

Some high schools—such as Green Hope High School in Cary, North Carolina, in the United States—are beginning to offer ethical hacking courses. Students learn about major cybersecurity incidents, the need for skilled professional hackers to battle cybercriminals, the types of common cybercrimes, and key cybersecurity skills, such as penetration testing. Many high schools have computer clubs, and some have hacking clubs.

Other high school classes that will help you to prepare for a career in computer security include:

- mathematics
- English and speech
- foreign language
- business, marketing, and accounting (if you plan to start your own company)

APPRENTICESHIPS

When most people think of apprenticeships, they think of electrician or carpentry apprenticeships. But did you know that apprenticeships are available in hundreds of careers, including computer security?

In 2015, the Community Initiative Center of Excellence for Secure Software launched the first **registered apprenticeship** program in cybersecurity in the United States. In this program, students attend Illinois Central College and participate in on-the-job training. Those who complete the program earn an associate's of applied science in secure software development. Courses in this program include:

An instructor (seated at center) offers cybersecurity tips to two apprentices.

- Computer Science
- Programming in Java
- Intro to Computer Security
- Intro to Relational Databases
- C#
- Secure Coding
- Mobile Application Programming
- Structured Query Language
- Intro to Assured Software Engineering
- Database Administration
- Structured System Analysis

Another cybersecurity apprenticeship program is offered at Coastline Community College in Garden Grove, California. The program lasts about one and a half years. In addition to coursework, apprentices complete 2,000 hours of paid, on-the-job training. Classes in this program include:

- Intro to Security (Security+)
- Network+ CST
- Server+ CIS
- Intro to Python Programming
- Ethical Hacking
- Computer Forensics
- Cybersecurity Analyst+
- CompTIA Linux+

Participating in an apprenticeship is an excellent way to prepare for a career because, unlike college, you do not have to pay tuition and you do receive a salary.

Learn more about a boot camp for high school students who are interested in white hat hacking

TYPES OF EDUCATION CREDENTIALS

A **certificate** shows that a person has completed specialized education, passed a test, and met other requirements to qualify for work in a career or industry. College certificate programs typically last six months to a year.

A student earns an **associate's degree** after they complete two years of post–high school education at a community or technical college.

A student earns a **bachelor's degree** in one of two ways:

- by earning an associate's degree and completing two additional years of education at a four-year college or university
- by graduating from high school and completing four years of education at a four-year college or university.

A **master's degree** is a graduate-level credential that is awarded to a student after they first complete a four-year bachelor's degree, then complete two additional years of education.

A student earns a doctoral degree after first earning a bachelor's and master's degree. To earn a doctorate, students must conduct original research, prepare a dissertation (a type of long report), and defend their dissertation before a committee of professors.

COLLEGES AND UNIVERSITIES

You'll need at least an associate's degree, but preferably a bachelor's degree, to enter this field. To be eligible for managerial and executive positions, many employers require applicants to have a master's degree. It's important to earn a degree. Four out of five cybersecurity jobs require a college degree, according to the National Cyber Security Alliance.

Many colleges and universities offer degrees in cybersecurity. In the United States, about twenty of these programs have been designed to meet the standards of the National Centers of Academic Excellence in Cyber Defense. Several of these programs have concentrations in secure software development. While attending such a college does not guarantee that you'll get a job, it will

A professor discusses cybersecurity attack response protocols with two students.

certainly look good on your **resume**. You can a view a list of the schools at www.nsa.gov/resources/students-educators/centers-academic-excellence/ cae-co-centers.shtml. Other countries have similar centers that work with colleges to develop cybersecurity programs.

You can also prepare for this field by earning a degree in computer science, software development, network management, and other computer-related fields. Those who pursue this route usually earn a certificate in computer security and/or ethical hacking. Schools that offer certificates in ethical hacking include the University of Washington, Southern Methodist University in Texas, and Thomas Nelson Community College in Virginia.

Topics covered in cybersecurity education include pentesting; network security; risk assessment and forensics; ethical hacking; managing the implementation and maintenance of security devices, systems, procedures and countermeasures; and organizational prevention, detection, countering, and recovery methods. College students typically complete at least one **internship** as part of their training.

GLOBAL INDUSTRIES MOST TARGETED BY CYBER-ESPIONAGE

Cyber-espionage occurs when cybercriminals use the internet or other technology to steal classified or sensitive data or intellectual property to gain an advantage over a company or government. The following industries were the most common target in 2017, according to Statista.com:

1. Public sector (the part of the economy that is controlled by the government)

2. Manufacturing

3. Professional (accounting, law, engineering, etc.)

4. Health care

5. Education

6. Financial information

7. Hotels

The health-care industry is a major target of cyber-espionage.

MILITARY

Wars are no longer just fought with bullets and missiles. These days, teams of hackers are training to wage war against an enemy's tanks, ships, and submarines, as well as attack a country's electric, water, and other systems. For example, an unknown person, organization, or country launched the Stuxnet Worm in 2010 against Iran's nuclear facilities, which some believed were developing nuclear weapons. This caused significant damage to the Iranian nuclear program.

The Stuxnet Worm and other examples of cyberwarfare show that militaries around the world need professional hackers and other cybersecurity professionals to both defend systems against cyberattack and develop software that can be used to attack opposing armies and countries.

Four U.S. military branches (Air Force, Coast Guard, Marines, and Navy), as well as many militaries in other countries, provide training for information security analysts. In the military, you'll learn how to use computers and peripheral equipment (if you don't already know how); plan, design, and test computer systems; write code; debug systems; and protect computers from hackers, among other skills. While you train, you'll receive a salary and will not have to pay any tuition, but you will have to make a service commitment of two to four years. Ask your recruiter for more information.

The military offers other computer-related careers that can be a starting point for entering the computer security field. Additionally, some people become professional hackers after working in military intelligence.

DAY IN THE LIFE: PROFESSIONAL HACKER AT A PENETRATION TESTING COMPANY

I work at a fast-growing penetration testing and digital security company. I perform a variety of penetration tests where I attempt to hack into accounts of customers using malware and other techniques. But some companies want us to try to sneak into their facilities to test their physical security. I have to admit that this is my favorite aspect of my job. I minored in drama in college, and I've always enjoyed acting, doing funny voices, and impersonating famous people on Halloween.

On a typical job, I start my day by dressing up in a spiffy business suit in order to pretend that I'm an executive at the company. I also have to convey a certain attitude as I walk through the lobby of the building. I present myself as hyperconfident and important. I even act a little cocky, as if I would be surprised if someone decided to stop me as I walk into the offices of the company. I stand up straight, hold my head high, and send the message that I belong at this company—even if I don't. I'll usually enter the building in the morning when everyone is arriving to start their day, or at lunchtime or breaks, when many workers are coming and going from the building. I've created a fake badge that mimics what I saw company employees wearing during previous surveillance missions.

If I get past security, I walk into the office (still with my confident and cocky attitude) and look for an empty office or workstation where I can set up my laptop and try to hack into the company's systems. I've done a lot of research on company employees and departments, so if I'm questioned, I'm ready to drop names and present a story of why I'm there. If everything goes well, I'll hack into the company's computers. I might also plug in a USB drive that installs an undetectable bot that will capture information or damage a system, and take photos and videos of server rooms, proprietary systems, and other areas that would be useful to a potential cybercriminal.

I try other ways to sneak into the company. I might simply climb a fence after office hours and seek to open various doors to see if any are unlocked. Or I might tailgate a car in front of me to get past the need to use an entry pass. There are many ways to try to bypass security.

Things don't always go well. Some companies have excellent security and I never make it past the security desk in the lobby. Or I'm caught red-handed as I sit at a cubicle attempting to hack into the company's systems. I carry a "get out of jail free" letter from my employer to explain who I am and that I have permission to perform penetration testing. But I don't use it often. It's amazing how lax physical security is at some companies, and how trusting people are if you wear a nice suit and act like you belong!

GETTING A JOB

You're probably not ready to start a career in cybersecurity, but it's never too early to learn how the job search process works. After all, the more you know about using job boards, networking, accessing resources from professional associations, and other job search tools, the better off you'll be when it comes time to look for your first job. You can also use these resources to help find an internship while you're in college. Here are some popular job search methods for job hunters.

MAJOR EMPLOYERS OF PROFESSIONAL HACKERS

- Companies (banks, utilities, hospitals, etc.)
- Nonprofit organizations
- Colleges and universities
- Government agencies
- Military
- Computer security research facilities

The multi-trillion-dollar financial industry is a major employer of professional hackers.

Your high school computer science teacher is just one member of your network.

USE YOUR NETWORK

You probably know what a computer network is—a group of interconnected computers that communicate with each other and perform tasks. But did you know that there are other types of networks that you can use to get an internship or job, or achieve other life goals? It might come as a surprise that you already have a network! Your personal network consists of your family, friends, and classmates. It comes in handy when you miss a day of school and need a classmate's science notes, or if you want to learn more about tryouts for your school's soccer team. Your personal network may eventually help you land your first after-school job. Once you get to college, you'll also become part of a professional network that includes your professors, internship directors, coaches, bosses, classmates, and people you meet online, including at social networking sites such as LinkedIn.

Networking—especially professional networking—may seem overwhelming, but it's really not. It just involves talking with people, making new friends, exchanging information, and helping others when they need assistance.

CHECK OUT JOB BOARDS

Internet job boards are a popular way to apply for and land internships and jobs. They are offered by professional associations, government agencies, businesses, and other organizations. While you're probably a few years from applying for an internship or job, it's a good idea to check out some job listings to see what types of education and skills are in demand. Here are a few computer security job boards:

- www.csoonline.com/jobs
- https://cybersecurityventures.com/career-news
- https://cybersecjobs.com

And here are some job sites that offer computer security job listings:

- www.indeed.com
- www.linkedin.com
- www.dice.com
- www.cybercareers.gov/job-seeker (U.S. government job board)
- www.jobbank.gc.ca (Canadian government job board)
- www.gov.uk/jobsearch (United Kingdom government job board)

JOIN AND USE THE RESOURCES OF PROFESSIONAL ASSOCIATIONS

Professional associations offer a wealth of career exploration and job search resources for aspiring professional hackers. They provide membership (including categories for students), training opportunities, job listings, networking events, and certification. Certification is a credential that you earn by passing a test and meeting other requirements. It's very important in the computer security industry. Those who become certified have a better chance of landing a job and earning good pay than those who are not certified.

If you're looking for a job—or just want to learn more about a career or industry—association websites should be some of your first stops. Here are some major professional associations for computer security workers around the world:

- Australian Information Security Association: https://aisa.org.au
- EC-Council: www.eccouncil.org
- High Technology Crime Investigation Association: www.htcia.org
- Information Systems Security Association: www.issa.org
- InfoSecurity Ireland: www.infosecurityireland.org
- (ISC)^2: www.isc2.org
- New Zealand Security Association: https://security.org.nz
- SANS Institute: www.sans.org
- Security Analysis and Risk Management Association: http://sarma.org
- UK Cyber Security Association: https://cybersecurityassociation.co.uk

SALARIES FOR INFORMATION SECURITY ANALYSTS BY U.S. STATE

Earnings for information security analysts vary by state based on demand and other factors. Here are the five states where employers pay the highest average salary and the states in which employers pay the lowest salaries.

Highest Average Salaries:
1. New Jersey: $120,020
2. New York: $118,140
3. Virginia: $110,450
4. Maine: $110,080
5. California: $108,090

Lowest Average Salaries:
1. Montana: $60,000
2. Wyoming: $72,180
3. Mississippi: $75,500
4. Oklahoma: $75,760
5. North Dakota: $76,070

Source: U.S. Department of Labor

HOW MUCH CAN I EARN?

Earnings for professional hackers and other computer security professionals vary by job title, educational background, the worker's experience level, whether they work full or part time, and other factors. For example, a professional hacker with five years of experience will make more money than someone who is just starting out in their first job after college. Certified professional hackers make

Certified ethical hackers earn average salaries of $89,000, according to PayScale.com.

more money than hackers who are not certified. Managers usually earn higher salaries than the people whom they supervise.

Those who work in computer security earn much higher salaries than those who work in many other careers. PayScale.com reports that certified ethical hackers earn average salaries of $89,000. The lowest paid workers earn $54,215, while the highest paid hackers earn $113,803.

Data security analysts earn salaries that range from $113,500 to $160,000, according to Robert Half Technology.

The median annual salary for information security analysts (who have both hacker and non-hacker duties) is $95,510, according to the U.S. Department of Labor. The lowest paid professionals earn less than $55,560 per year, and the highest earners receive $153,090 or more per year.

Here are average salary ranges for other computer security specialties, according to RHT:

- chief security officer: $143,250–$241,000
- information systems security manager: $115,250–$194,250
- network security administrator: $92,000–$155,000
- network security engineer: $97,000–$163,000
- systems security administrator: $92,750–$156,000

Computer security professionals who work full time (35–40 hours a week) for government agencies, companies, and other organizations often receive fringe benefits such as health insurance, paid vacation and sick days, and other perks. Self-employed workers—those who work for themselves, rather than for an employer—do not receive these benefits.

TEXT-DEPENDENT QUESTIONS:

1. What are some typical college classes for those who want to become a computer security specialist?
2. What are the benefits of joining computer security associations?
3. How much can professional hackers earn?

RESEARCH PROJECT:

Interview professional hackers who trained for the field via an apprenticeship, college, and the military. Ask them what they liked and disliked about this training method and what they would do differently if they could repeat their training. Create a chart that lists the pros and cons of each educational approach. Which is the best approach for you?

WORDS TO UNDERSTAND

crowdsourcing: the process of using large groups of people—usually on the internet—to accomplish a goal

infrastructure: the systems of a city, region, or nation, such as communication, sewage, water, transportation, bridges, dams, and electric

nonprofit organization: a group that uses any profits it generates to advance its stated goals (protecting the environment, helping the homeless, etc.); it is not a corporation or other for-profit business

Chapter 4

KEY SKILLS AND METHODS OF EXPLORATION

SKILL BUILDING LEADS TO SUCCESS

Many people believe that all you need to be successful as a professional hacker are good programming and other technical skills. But there's a lot more to this job than just being a whiz with computers. You'll also need **soft skills**, such as the ability to communicate effectively, manage time, solve problems, and work as a member of a team. Here are some key traits for professional hackers.

PROBLEM-SOLVING AND ANALYTICAL SKILLS

A complex cyberattack is like a difficult puzzle that must be solved in steps. Professional hackers must have good problem-solving and analytical abilities to know what steps to take to solve the problem. The most successful professional hackers are curious about how things work and enjoy tinkering until they find a solution to a problem.

IMAGINATION AND CREATIVITY

Professional hackers need to think like cybercriminals. They need to imagine the goals of the cybercriminal—stealing sensitive information, attacking a website so it no longer works correctly, or spreading malware so that tens of thousands of computers are affected around the world. They also need to envision how the cybercriminal will go about meeting these goals, and what they will do if their first attempts at cybercrime are blocked. Professional hackers also need creativity in order to develop new tools and strategies to stop cybercrime.

TECHNICAL SKILLS

You'll need to be very familiar with popular programming languages (C++, Python, Java, PHP, Perl, etc.), network protocols/services, and penetration testing and cyberattack prevention tools. You should also be familiar with Windows, Linux, Android, Unix, and other operating systems. To be successful in this career, you'll need to constantly update your skills because technology and cybercrime strategies are always changing.

ETHICS

Companies and other organizations place great trust in professional hackers when they hire them to analyze and hack their systems. Massive amounts of top secret information, financial or personal data, or the successful operation of public electric systems, national security systems, and other critical **infrastructure** are at risk when a professional hacker does their work. They must keep their findings private and resist the urge to sell this information to cybercriminals. If you engage in black hat hacking, you could go to jail. And if you manage to avoid jail, you'll probably never work as a white hat hacker again

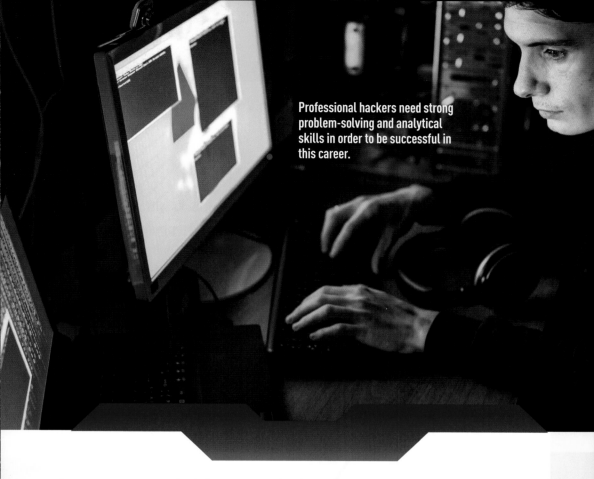

Professional hackers need strong problem-solving and analytical skills in order to be successful in this career.

because most security jobs require a background check and participation in a polygraph test.

COMMUNICATION AND INTERPERSONAL SKILLS

Professional hackers often work as members of a team, so it's important to be able to communicate effectively—especially during a cyberattack—in order to address the issue quickly. Professional hackers need good writing skills because they must prepare detailed reports about security vulnerabilities and explain the steps they took to address these issues or respond to a cyberattack. They frequently provide reports and updates to company executives, who may have little or no technical knowledge. Being able to explain technical jargon to non-techies is an important skill.

PATIENCE AND TENACITY

In the movies, professional hackers often thwart cyberattacks with a few keystrokes in a matter of minutes. But this is not a realistic representation of the challenging work of professional hackers. Countering most cyberattacks takes more than just a few minutes, and professional hackers need to be calm under pressure and be patient because their first (or second, or third) response against a cyberattack may not work.

BUSINESS SKILLS

If you plan to launch a cybersecurity business, you'll quickly need to become an expert in basic accounting, marketing, social media, bidding on jobs, managing staff, and performing other tasks that keep your company running smoothly.

HOW TO STOP A HACKER

It's important to take precautions to keep your computer, smartphone, or other technology from being hacked. Do the following to stay safe online:

- **Never use the same password.** If you use the same password, a hacker will feast on your online accounts if they get your password. If you have trouble remembering passwords, use free password management services such as LastPass and KeePass.

- **Make your password long and complex**. Use a combination of uppercase and lowercase letters, numbers, and special characters.

Don't use your address, phone number, or birthdate in your password.

- **Set up two-factor security for important accounts.** This type of security creates two different password or verification stages before you can access your account.

- **Be very careful when clicking links on websites and emails.** Many websites now have the "https" moniker, which stands for "Hyper Text Transfer Protocol Secure," and it means that all communications between you and this website are encrypted.

- **Activate as many privacy settings as you can on social media accounts.** Otherwise, you're just handing information to cybercriminals.

- **Lie.** It's never right to lie...except when you're attempting to thwart hackers. Security experts suggest that people create false answers to security questions such as "What city were you born in?" and "What is your father's middle name?" to confuse potential hackers who might search publicly available information to try to hack you.

- **Keep your WiFi turned off when you're not using it.** This reduces your chances of being hacked.

- **Steer clear of public wireless networks that do not require a password.**

- **Be sure to install anti-virus software and make sure it is up to date.**

- **Pick up the phone if you encounter the unknown.** If you receive a questionable email or text message from a friend or school contact, don't respond digitally. Instead, call the contact to see if they sent you the message.

- **Use file backup software.** That way, if you are hacked, you'll be able to recover your files.

Taking computer science classes in high school is an excellent way to learn more about cybersecurity.

EXPLORING CYBERSECURITY AS A STUDENT

There are many ways to learn more about cybersecurity and careers in the field. Here are some popular methods of exploration.

TAKE A CLASS

You've taken plenty of computer classes in middle school or high school, but did you know that college and universities, professional associations, government agencies, and other organizations offer cybersecurity courses, both in person and online? These classes are a good way to learn more about cybersecurity. One great example are the free, online classes offered by Hacker Highschool (www.hackerhighschool.org). It offers the following classes in English and eleven other languages: Being a Hacker, Essential Commands, Beneath the Internet, Playing With Daemons, System Identification, Hacking Malware, Attack Analysis, Forensics, Hacking Email, Web Security and Privacy, Hacking Passwords, and Defensive Hacking. All you have to do is visit the Hacker Highschool website, download and read the class guides, and complete the exercises. Your cybersecurity knowledge will increase in no time!

Here are a few other classes to check out:

- Heimdal Security (https://cybersecuritycourse.co): Cyber Security for Beginners

- CodeHS (https://codehs.com/info/curriculum/cybersecurity): Cybersecurity

- iD Tech (www.idtech.com/courses/cybersecurity-and-encryption): Cybersecurity and Encryption

- hackerone (www.hackerone.com/hacker101): Hacker101

PROFILE: A REFORMED BLACK HAT HACKER

I tricked people into giving me their private information. I hacked into their computers to steal credit card numbers. And I even participated in a denial-of-service attack that shut down the website of a government agency. I'm not bragging. I'm ashamed of my past behavior. I used to be a black hat hacker, but that was in the past. Today, I'm a white hat hacker for a government agency. Part of my plea deal with the authorities was to provide information to the government about how I and others hacked into government systems.

My hacking career started when I was fourteen. I'd get together with friends and we'd play massively multiplayer online games. At first it was just fun competing, but then we tried to hack the system to get freebies. We were amazed at how easy it was to hack some of the games. I was so into video games that my grades started to slip. An idea occurred to me: Why not hack into my high school's computer system and change a few of my grades? I cringe now at the thought, but I did it. I changed Ds to Cs, and even gave myself an A in biology (my toughest subject). I started participating in legal bug bounty programs for Google, Amazon, and other companies, and began making money. It was thrilling to hack into systems, and I wanted more...and more. I wanted to hack bigger targets. A friend told me about the deep web, and soon I was working for black hat organizations that were illegally hacking software developers, the average person, and government agencies.

I worked as a black hat hacker for a few years, but while the work was exciting and I earned a lot of money, I began to feel bad inside. A few of my friends told me that they'd been hacked. One friend even had her identity stolen online, ruining her reputation. Listening to their stories made me see the damage that I was causing. Real people were being hurt, and it bothered me. Yet I kept on working as a black hat for a few more months until I got caught by the Federal Bureau of Investigation. I can't tell you how I got caught, but I can tell you that I felt relieved when it happened. A big weight fell from my shoulders. Although I had to serve three months in jail and pay a fine of $20,000, a government agency so valued my hacking skills that it offered me a position as a white hat hacker. Not everyone is as lucky as me. Some black hat hackers face years in jail and never work as hackers again.

If you love hacking, do the right thing and never become a black hat hacker. Resist the urge to cheat at games, change your grades, and otherwise use technology to break the rules. It's a slippery slope—one day you're hacking games as a teenager, and in time you're committing a serious crime that could result in jail time. It's just as fun to work for the good guys, and you'll sleep better at night, too.

ATTEND A CYBERSECURITY SUMMER CAMP

At a cybersecurity camp, you'll get the chance to learn about hacking, penetration testing, malware and other common types of computer attacks, and much more. These camps are offered by cybersecurity associations, government agencies, colleges, high schools, community groups, companies, and other organizations. More general camps that teach you about software development and other computer fields are also available. Your high school counselor or computer teacher can direct you toward camps in your area, or you can find opportunities by doing a keyword search on the internet.

Here are several examples of well-known camps in the United States and Canada. Camps are also available in other countries.

GENCYBER (WWW.GEN-CYBER.COM/CAMPS)

GenCyber summer camps are open to K–12 students throughout the United States. The goals of these camps are to increase student interest in cybersecurity careers and make the cybersecurity workforce more diverse, teach students about safe and appropriate online behavior, and educate campers about cybersecurity basics and hacking defense techniques. There is no cost to attend these camps. Funding is provided by the National Security Agency and the National Science Foundation.

CYBERPATRIOT (WWW.USCYBERPATRIOT.ORG)

CyberPatriot is the National Youth Cyber Education Program created by the Air Force Association to inspire K–12 students to pursue careers in cybersecurity or other science, technology, engineering, and mathematics disciplines. It offers five-day CyberCamps that are both fun and informative. Standard and Advanced CyberCamps are available.

DIGITAL MEDIA ACADEMY (WWW.DIGITALMEDIAACADEMY.ORG)

The academy offers a one-week Cybersecurity & Ethical Hacking Camp for young people ages twelve to seventeen at locations throughout the United States and

A professional hacker provides advice on protecting yourself from cybercriminals

Canada. In this camp, you'll learn the basics of scripting using Python; how to create, encode, and decode ciphers; analyze a network for information, and much more. The academy is sponsored by the Stanford University Continuing Studies Department.

FINDING MORE CAMPS

Many other colleges, organizations, and businesses offer summer cybersecurity and general computer science camps. Contact schools and organizations in your area to learn more.

JOIN THE TECHNOLOGY STUDENT ASSOCIATION

If you're a middle school or high school student and interested in science, technology, engineering, and mathematics, consider joining the Technology Student Association (TSA, www.tsaweb.org). This national **nonprofit organization** offers sixty competitions at its annual conference—including those in coding, software development, video game design, system control

A sailor helps a high school student complete cybersecurity challenges during a CyberThon event at Naval Air Station Pensacola.

technology, and technology problem-solving. The TSA also provides opportunities to develop your leadership skills and compete for money for college. Ask your school counselor or science teacher if your school has a TSA chapter and, if not, ask them to start one.

PARTICIPATE IN A COMPETITION

Competing in a hacking contest is a good way to build your skills. International, national, and regional associations; corporations; schools; and other organizations sponsor such contests. Check out the following competitions:

NATIONAL CYBER LEAGUE

The National Cyber League (NCL) provides a cybersecurity training ground for high school and college students. Students compete in events that simulate actual challenges faced by cybersecurity professionals. High school students get to compete in a capture-the-flag–style cybersecurity competition in which they simultaneously attack an opponent's computer defenses while protecting their own systems. At the end of the competition, players receive an NCL Scouting Report, which identifies their strengths and weaknesses. Some students include their NCL stats in their resumes to demonstrate their interest and skill in cybersecurity. Learn more at www.nationalcyberleague.org.

NATIONAL YOUTH CYBER DEFENSE COMPETITION

This competition, which is sponsored by the Air Force Association, puts teams of high school and middle school students in the position of newly hired information technology professionals who are responsible for managing a company's computer network. During rounds of competition, "teams are given a set of virtual images that represent operating systems and are tasked with finding cybersecurity vulnerabilities within the images and hardening the system while maintaining critical services." Teams compete at the state and regional levels, and top teams compete in the National Finals Competition to earn fame and fortune (aka scholarship money). Learn more at www. uscyberpatriot.org.

MAGIC CAPTURE THE FLAG COMPETITION

MAGIC (Mid-Atlantic Gigabit Innovation Collaboratory) is a nonprofit organization in Westminster, Maryland, that works to encourage young people to pursue careers in cybersecurity. Each year, it offers an entry-level ethical hacking cybersecurity competition for high school and college students. This competition not only offers participants a chance to test their skills against other hackers, it's also a great way to meet others who are interested in cybersecurity. Learn more at https://magicinc.org.

SKILLSUSA

SkillsUSA is a national membership organization for middle school, high school, and college students who are preparing for careers in technical, trade, and skilled service occupations. It doesn't offer a hacking competition, but it does offer competitions for those who are interested in computers. Competitions include Computer Programming, Interactive Application and Video Game Design, Internetworking, Technical Computer Applications, and Web Design. SkillsUSA does offer Cyber Security as a demonstration event (not a competition). Participants demonstrate their ability to protect computer systems from cyberthreats, recognize risks, respond to cyberattacks, and recover damaged or compromised systems. Perhaps Cyber Security will someday be added as a competition. SkillsUSA works directly with high schools and colleges, so ask your school counselor or teacher if it is an option for you. Learn more at www. skillsusa.org.

Additional competitions can be discovered at CyberCompEx, www.cybercompex. org/category/competitions.

COLLEGE COMPETITIONS

Once you get to college, check out the following cybersecurity competitions:

- National Collegiate Cyber Defense Competition: www.nationalccdc.org
- Global Cyberlympics: www.cyberlympics.org

Learn more about the National Collegiate Cyber Defense Competition

BUG HUNTING FACTS

In 2017, Bugcrowd, a leader in security testing via **crowdsourcing**, conducted a survey to learn more about people who hunt for computer bugs. Here are some of its findings:

- 71 percent of bug hunters were eighteen to twenty-nine years old, up from 60 percent in 2016.

- 82 percent had completed some form of higher education; 16 percent held a master's degree or higher.

- 44 percent of bug hunters said that the main reason why they liked bug hunting was for "the challenge."

- 27 percent said that they wanted to become full-time bug hunters.

FIND A BUG!

Your goal in this exploration activity is not to find an ant or a wasp, but to find a glitch or another problem with software. If a bug is not fixed by a software developer, it can be exploited by cybercriminals. Many companies provide cash rewards to ethical hackers who identify bugs that, if not fixed, could result in the theft of secret product information or financial data, or that could cause damage to its computer systems.

It can really pay to be a bug hunter. For example, in 2018, Google awarded a Uruguayan teenager a "bug bounty" of more than $36,000 for detecting a security flaw in one of its programs. CNBC.com reports that Google awarded $2.9 million to 274 different bug hunters in 2017, with a top award of $112,500. Looking for computer bugs might bring you a cash award, but it's also a good

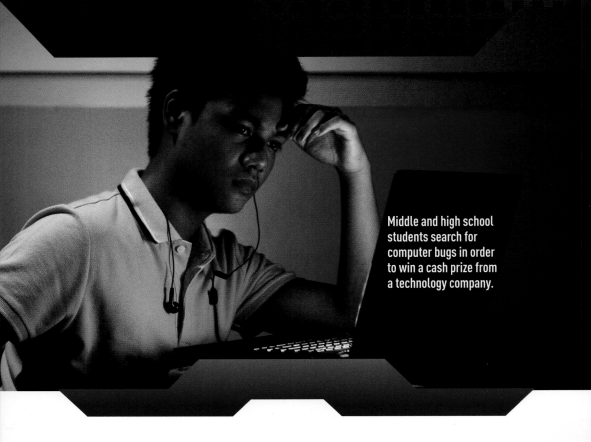

Middle and high school students search for computer bugs in order to win a cash prize from a technology company.

way to develop your skills and become known in the industry (if you happen to find a bug in a well-known product).

Here are a few examples of bug bounty programs to check out:

- GitHub Security Bug Bounty: https://bounty.github.com
- Google Vulnerability Reward Program: www.google.com/about/appsecurity/reward-program
- United Airlines Bug Bounty Program: www.united.com/ual/en/us/fly/contact/bugbounty.html
- Hackerone: www.hackerone.com/internet-bug-bounty (more opportunities)

SOURCES OF ADDITIONAL EXPLORATION

Contact the following organizations for more information on education and careers in the cybersecurity industry, certification, and membership:

Association for Computing Machinery
www.acm.org

CompTIA
www.comptia.org

EC-Council
www.eccouncil.org

High Technology Crime Investigation Association
www.htcia.org

IEEE Computer Society
www.computer.org

Information Systems Security Association
www.issa.org

(ISC)²
www.isc2.org

National Initiative for Cybersecurity Careers and Studies
http://niccs.us-cert.gov

SANS Institute
www.sans.org

Security Analysis and Risk Management Association
http://sarma.org

JOIN THE SCOUTS

The Boy Scouts and Girl Scouts are membership organizations for boys and girls ages roughly five to eighteen (age ranges vary by country and group). These organizations help you to be a better citizen and person, and teach you all kinds of things that you didn't know before. When you learn something new in scouts, you usually receive a merit badge or other type of award.

If you are a boy or a girl in the United States, you can join the Boy Scouts of America (www.scouting.org) and earn merit badges in Digital Technology, Electronics, and Game Design. A Cybersecurity merit badge is currently in development. Members of the Girl Scouts of the United States of America (www.girlscouts.org) can earn a variety of cybersecurity merit badges based on their age level.

You don't have to live in the United States to be a scout. In fact, the Boy Scouts were founded in Great Britain more than 100 years ago. Scouting organizations in Great Britain include The Scout Association (https://scouts.org.uk) and British Boy Scouts and British Girl Scouts Association (https://bbsandbgs.org.uk). If you live in Canada, you can join Scouts Canada (www.scouts.ca).

INTERVIEW A PROFESSIONAL HACKER

You can learn more about careers in cybersecurity by participating in an information interview with a professional hacker or other type of computer security professional. In an information interview, you'll just ask a professional hacker questions about their job to learn more about the career.

Here are some questions to ask during the interview:

- Can you tell me about a day in your life on the job?

A professional hacker (right) uses a laptop to explain a cybersecurity concept during an information interview.

- What are the most important personal and professional qualities for people in your career?
- What do you like best and least about your job?
- Is your job stressful? If so, please explain why.
- What is the future employment outlook for professional hackers? How is the field changing?
- How did you prepare for this career?
- What can I do now to prepare for the field?

Your mom or dad, or perhaps a family friend, might know of a professional hacker who would be interested in discussing their career. Professional associations, the public relations departments of software companies, and your school counselor or computer science teacher can also help arrange an information interview.

TEXT-DEPENDENT QUESTIONS:

1. Why is it important for professional hackers to be patient?
2. What can you learn at a computer security summer camp?
3. What is information interviewing?

RESEARCH PROJECT:

Talk to professional hackers who work for government agencies, tech companies, and in the military. Ask them questions from the list in the information interviewing section. Write a report that compares and contrasts the job duties and educational requirements for each field.

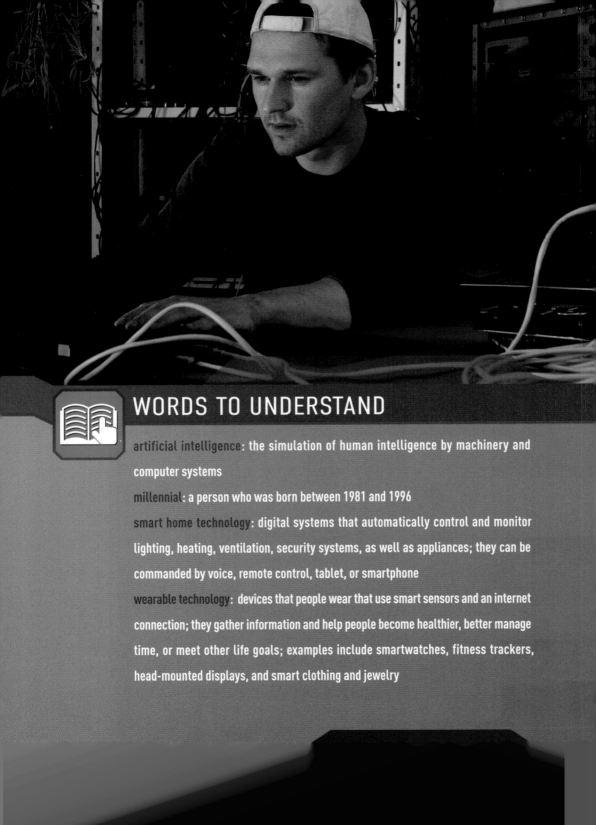

WORDS TO UNDERSTAND

artificial intelligence: the simulation of human intelligence by machinery and computer systems

millennial: a person who was born between 1981 and 1996

smart home technology: digital systems that automatically control and monitor lighting, heating, ventilation, security systems, as well as appliances; they can be commanded by voice, remote control, tablet, or smartphone

wearable technology: devices that people wear that use smart sensors and an internet connection; they gather information and help people become healthier, better manage time, or meet other life goals; examples include smartwatches, fitness trackers, head-mounted displays, and smart clothing and jewelry

Chapter 5

THE FUTURE OF DIGITAL SECURITY AND CAREERS IN THE FIELD

THE BIG PICTURE

Cybercrime is a very serious issue in the United States and throughout the world. Cybersecurity Ventures, a leading global cyber-economy research firm and publisher, estimates that cybercrime damages will cost the world $6 trillion annually by 2021. Cybercrime affects everyone—from individuals to companies, colleges and universities, government agencies, and the military. As a result, demand is strong for cybersecurity professionals. Employment of information security analysts (cybersecurity professionals who do the work of hackers and who have other duties) is expected to grow by 28 percent through 2026, according to the U.S. Department of Labor. "Organizations across industries like finance, retail, and education are looking for skilled professionals to design

A shortage of cybersecurity professionals is expected in Israel and other countries in the next decade.

and implement comprehensive information security that covers a wide range of business security priorities," advises Peninsula Press, a project of the Stanford Journalism Program.

Other sources also report strong demand for cybersecurity professionals. Robert Half Technology included the career of computer security professional on its list of "In-Demand Technology Roles for 2018." CyberSeek.com—a project of Burning Glass, CompTIA AITA, and the National Initiative for Cybersecurity Education—reports that demand is especially high for cybersecurity analysts, network engineers/architects, cybersecurity engineers, cybersecurity managers/ administrators, software developers/engineers, systems engineers, systems administrators, vulnerability analysts/penetration testers, and information technology auditors.

Opportunities will also be strong outside the United States. In fact:

- India will need 1 million cybersecurity professionals by 2020, according to the National Association of Software and Services Companies.

- Israel, Australia, France, Germany, Japan, the United Kingdom, and Mexico are expected to experience a shortage of cybersecurity professionals in coming years, according to a survey by Intel Corp.

- There will be a shortage of 350,000 cybersecurity workers in Europe by 2022, according to a survey by the information security certification body (ISC)[2].

DAY IN THE LIFE: PROFESSIONAL HACKER

I'm a professional hacker at a software company. I've been a hacker for about ten years. I actually worked as a computer science teacher for five years before deciding to switch careers to a higher-paying field because I got married and wanted to start a family.

A typical workday begins on my way to work. I take the train into our company's headquarters and fill my commute by scanning cybersecurity-oriented posts on my Twitter account, blogs, and news sites to see what's new. Perhaps there's a story about new vulnerabilities or attacks. If I spot something of interest, I'll look into it myself once I get to work or have a member of my team investigate. It's important to stay ahead of the curve when it comes to cybersecurity because you can't play catch-up when a cyberattack is under way.

The rest of my day consists of managing employees (many of whom work remotely), conducting penetration tests to determine weaknesses in our software, fixing those issues, and meeting with company executives and coworkers regarding any ongoing cyberattacks or vulnerability issues that we've identified. I also spend a lot of time building new security tools.

I like this career because each day is different. There are always new things to learn, new types of attacks, and new types of solutions. We're constantly developing new products, which keeps me on my toes. It might sound strange to say is, but this job is really fun. I enjoy solving problems and stopping hackers in their tracks.

But despite strong demand for cybersecurity professionals, there is a shortage of qualified workers. Cybersecurity Ventures predicts that there will be a worldwide shortage of 3.5 million cybersecurity workers by 2021. A major factor behind this shortage is the fact that few younger people want to pursue a career in cybersecurity. Only 9 percent of **millennials** who were surveyed by ProtectWise and Enterprise Strategy Group in 2018 reported that they were interested in pursuing a career in cybersecurity. Those surveyed were familiar with information technology careers (for example, 33 percent wanted to pursue a career in video game development), but they seemed unaware of the great opportunities in cybersecurity. Only 17 percent of respondents said that someone in their family had worked in cybersecurity. Sixty-nine percent said they had never taken a cybersecurity class in school, and 65 percent said that their school did not offer cybersecurity courses. It's clear that more has to be done to educate young people about cybersecurity. A 2017 report from the computer association (ISC)² found that only 7 percent of cybersecurity workers were under age twenty-nine.

So other than not being aware of cybersecurity careers, why aren't young people entering this field? Some young people believe that the field is boring, low-paying, and lacks opportunities for career advancement. These beliefs are untrue. The following statistics bust these myths:

- *U.S. News & World Report* ranked the career of information security analyst as the 32nd best job (out of hundreds of careers) in the United States because it offers a combination of good pay, relatively low stress, challenging work, advancement possibilities, and strong employment demand.

- A wide variety of job opportunities are available in cybersecurity. The U.S. Department of Homeland Security reports that there are more than thirty different types of cybersecurity work—from digital forensics to systems security analysis.

- PayScale.com reports that certified ethical hackers earn average salaries of $89,000. The lowest paid workers earn $54,215, while

Learn about the future of cyberwarfare

the highest paid hackers earn $113,803. Data security analysts earn salaries that range from $102,000 to $171,500, according to Robert Half Technology. These salary figures are much higher than the average salary ($50,620) for all workers in the United States.

GOOD NEWS

Seventy percent of teens ages thirteen to seventeen who were surveyed in 2017 for the CompTIA report, *Youth Opinions of Careers in Information Technology*, said that they were open to the possibility of a career in the tech industry. That's an increase of 8 percent from 2015.

The introduction of wearable technology has created many more opportunities for black hat hackers to steal people's private information and commit other cybercrimes.

CHALLENGES TO EMPLOYMENT GROWTH

Demand for professional hackers is very strong, but there a few trends that could slow employment growth. If computer security becomes automated (with the help of **artificial intelligence**), demand will decline for cybersecurity professionals. But there is no existing technology that can stop cyberattacks, so professional hackers should not expect to be replaced by computers anytime soon. And even if this occurs, there will still be a need for cybersecurity professionals to monitor automated systems and develop new security systems and tools. Additionally, software is increasingly being introduced into our homes (via **smart home technology**), vehicles (ABI predicts that more than 20 million connected cars with built-in software-based security technology will be produced by 2020), implantable medical devices (pacemakers, insulin pumps, etc.), and wearable technology (half a billion **wearable devices** will be sold worldwide in 2021, according to the Herjavec Group). These devices make life easier, but they also increase opportunities for cybercriminals to steal our personal information, or even use technology to hurt us by tampering with pacemakers or by taking over and crashing our cars. The vast amount of internet-connected technology that is being introduced suggests that cybercriminals will find new ways to commit crimes and professional hackers will be needed to fight these cybercriminals.

WOMEN IN CYBERSECURITY

Although women comprise about 50 percent of the world population, only about 11 percent of cybersecurity professionals are female. This percentage is slightly higher in North America (14 percent) and much lower in the Middle East (5 percent). There are several reasons why more women do not pursue careers in cybersecurity, including high levels of discrimination, lack of advancement opportunities, and lower earnings than men. Fifty-one percent of women in the cybersecurity industry reported experiencing various forms of discrimination in the workplace. Only 15 percent of men in the cybersecurity industry reported that they had experienced discrimination. Men in the cybersecurity industry are four times more likely than women to hold executive-level positions, and women in non-managerial jobs earned $5,000 less a year than their male counterparts who were doing the same jobs.

The cybersecurity industry is attempting to increase the number of women who enter this field by hosting open houses, founding support groups, and establishing mentorship programs. Here are a few organizations that exist to support women in cybersecurity and other computer fields:

- Women in Cybersecurity: www.wicys.net

- Association for Women in Computing: www.awc-hq.org

- IEEE Computer Society-Women in Computing: www.computer.org/web/communities/women-in-computing

- National Center for Women & Information Technology: www.ncwit.org

Sources: The Center for Cyber Safety and Education, (ISC)², and Executive Women's Forum on Information Security, Risk Management & Privacy

THE FUTURE OF CYBERSECURITY

A lot has changed since the early days of cybersecurity. Cyberattacks can now be monitored and stopped in real-time. Artificial intelligence is being used to better predict and respond to cyberattacks. So what does the future hold for cybersecurity? Here are a few general trends that may occur:

- Artificial intelligence–powered security software will play a larger role in cybersecurity strategies. Artificial intelligence (AI) is the simulation of human intelligence by machinery and computer systems. AI-powered cybersecurity systems are developed to continually capture and analyze data in order to identify threats and analyze them before they can harm computers. Much of this technology is automated, which may reduce the need for cybersecurity workers—although experts disagree on how jobs will actually be affected.

- The world will become even more connected by technology, which will be incorporated into cars (including driverless vehicles), wearable technology, and homes. Many of the decisions we make now will be made automatically by computers, which suggests that automated technology could be exploited by cybercriminals.

There are many exciting opportunities for young women in the cybersecurity industry.

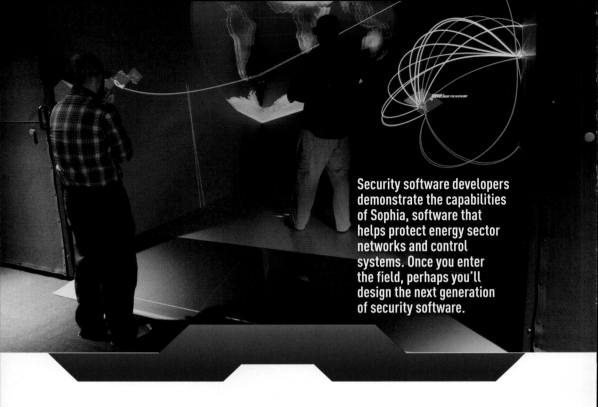

Security software developers demonstrate the capabilities of Sophia, software that helps protect energy sector networks and control systems. Once you enter the field, perhaps you'll design the next generation of security software.

- Cyberwarfare and cyber-espionage will become a larger part of each nation's offensive and defensive capabilities. Smaller countries with limited physical military resources will become cyberwar players because it is much cheaper to fight a cyberwar than a conventional war.

- As cybercrime becomes even more sophisticated, individuals, companies, and governments will need to spend more money to keep their systems safe from hackers.

IN CONCLUSION

Can you see yourself using the latest cutting-edge technology to fight cybercriminals? Do you have great technical skills and enjoy solving problems? Are you looking for a career that offers good pay and great job prospects? If so, then a career as a professional hacker could be in your future.

I hope that you'll use this book as a starting point to discover even more about this career. Talk to professional hackers and other cybersecurity professionals about their careers, use the resources of professional organizations, and most importantly, attend cybersecurity summer camps and try to win bug bounties to develop your skills. Good luck on your career exploration!

TEXT-DEPENDENT QUESTIONS:

1. Why is demand growing for cybersecurity professionals?
2. Why do some women avoid pursuing careers in cybersecurity?
3. What factors could slow career growth in cybersecurity?

RESEARCH PROJECT:

Spend some time exploring the future of cybersecurity. How will AI and other technologies change the work of professional hackers? Write a report about your findings and present it to your class.

PHOTO CREDITS

FURTHER READING

Beaver, Kevin. *Hacking For Dummies*. 6th ed. Hoboken, NJ: For Dummies, 2018.

Brooks, Charles J., Christopher Grow, Philip Craig, and Donald Short. *Cybersecurity Essentials*. Hoboken, NJ: Sybex, 2018.

Kaplan, Fred. *Dark Territory: The Secret History of Cyber War*. New York: Simon & Schuster, 2016.

LeClair, Jane, and Denise Pheils. *Women in Cybersecurity*. Albany, NY: Hudson Whitman/Excelsior College Press, 2016.

Sanger, David E. *The Perfect Weapon: War, Sabotage, and Fear in the Cyber Age*. London, UK: Scribe Publications, 2018.

INTERNET RESOURCES

www.bls.gov/ooh/computer-and-information-technology/information-security-analysts.htm: This section of the *Occupational Outlook Handbook* features information on job duties, educational requirements, salaries, and the employment outlook for information security analysts.

www.dhs.gov/sites/default/files/publications/cybersecurity-101_4.pdf: This site from the U.S. Department of Homeland Security offers an overview of cybersecurity and what you should do to stay safe in the event of a cyberattack.

https://insights.samsung.com/2017/07/26/cybersecurity-101-understanding-the-most-common-cyberattacks: A well-known information technology company provides details on the most common types of cyberattacks.

https://medium.com/@petershimming/a-brief-history-of-hacking-past-present-and-future-a5463bf3a764: Visit this swebsite for a brief history of hacking—from 1955 to the present day.

INDEX

EDUCATIONAL VIDEO LINKS

Chapter 1:
Learn more about the history of the internet and cybersecurity: http://x-qr.net/1FUA

Learn more about computer hacking, why people do it, and the types of hackers: http://x-qr.net/1HQ9

Chapter 3:
Learn more about a boot camp for high school students who are interested in white hat hacking: http://x-qr.net/1GTY

Chapter 4:
A professional hacker provides advice on protecting yourself from cybercriminals: http://x-qr.net/1D4V

Learn more about the National Collegiate Cyber Defense Competition: http://x-qr.net/1Hcz

Chapter 5:
Learn about the future of cyberwarfare: http://x-qr.net/1FBN

AUTHOR BIOGRAPHY

Andrew Morkes has been a writer and editor for more than twenty-five years. He is the author of more than 25 books about college-planning and careers, including all of the titles in this series, many titles in the Careers in the Building Trades series, the *Vault Career Guide to Social Media*, and *They Teach That in College!?: A Resource Guide to More Than 100 Interesting College Majors*, which was selected as one of the best books of the year by the library journal *Voice of Youth Advocates*. He is also the author and publisher of "The Morkes Report: College and Career Planning Trends" blog.